# A Book Of Wishes
# For You

*by Eve Merriam*
*Illustrated by Mary Tara O'Keefe*

The C.R. Gibson Company, Norwalk, Connecticut 06856

I wish
for you to know
that when you glance at the clock
to check the time
that is the exact moment
when
I am thinking of you.

I wish for your alarm clock
to awaken you with a sound
gentle as a rose petal.

May
your neighbor's radio
play
only music that
you request.

I wish for
a talking mynah bird
with silky plumage
and an iridescent beak

to perch
on a tree
outside
your bedroom

and every morning
when you awaken
there is the
magical bird on the bough

speaking the one word
the only word it knows
the one word it has been
trained to say
especially for you

and you hear the bird speaking
that one word
over and over
and sweetly over

the word is
happiness
happiness
happiness.

I wish that wherever
you walk in the woods
there will always be
a tree house.

May
wild strawberries
ripen
on your window sill.

May the washing machine
bring you
an extra sock.

I wish that
you will
never
lose one glove.

I wish for the rain in your life
to be gray and soft
as the feathers of a dove.

When you open
the bottom drawer of your desk
may there be
a piece of blue sky.

I wish that
along the flat dusty road
you will come upon
a crystalline waterfall.

On a cold windy day
may you be
nestled indoors
with a comforter
and a book and an apple
alongside.

I wish
that when you are
driving down the street
and there are no parking places

you drive around the block
and when you come around again
to the same street
suddenly

all the parking meters
send chiming sounds into the air
and the fire hydrants
fly away

and the bus stop signs
turn into
bouquets
of spring flowers

and you pluck a daffodil
and entwine it around
your steering wheel
as you park easily
with all the room in the world.

I wish that when you walk
in your new shoes
they will feel
as if
you are still wearing
your old ones.

May the line
you are standing in
be the one
that will
move ahead
first.

I wish for
your letter box
to overflow
with
non-junk mail.

May the next
telephone voice
you hear
be
live.

I wish for you
to learn to love darkness
as well as light,
for the tree
needs roots below
to grow up to the sky.

May you love
the child
that you were
and the person
you will grow to be.

When
you go into a restaurant
the menu will read:

"In honor of
your dining here
today's special dessert is

apple cinnamon pie
topped with cheese
topped with more apples
and more cinnamon

and strawberry long cake."
When you have finished eating it
there will be one more luscious berry

and triple chocolate fudge ice-cream
that with every spoonful
will make you an ounce thinner.

May you reach below the desert of
loneliness
to the deep flowing springs
of solitude.

I wish
for your umbrella
to fold up
into
a rainbow.

I wish
for you to find
that the key you lost
and gave up hope
of ever finding again
is in your inside pocket.

May you
open
the daily newspaper
and find
a heart-shaped lilac leaf.

May
tomorrow morning
be
an undiscovered island
for you
to explore.

I wish that above
the noise of traffic
you will hear
a singing bird.

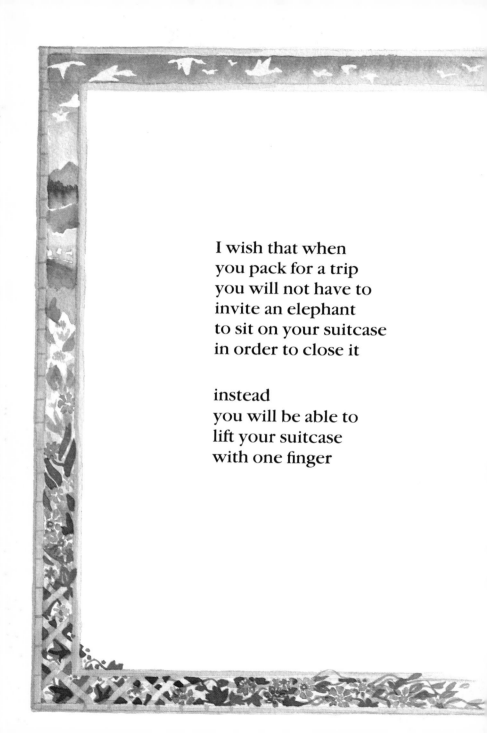

I wish that when
you pack for a trip
you will not have to
invite an elephant
to sit on your suitcase
in order to close it

instead
you will be able to
lift your suitcase
with one finger

because you will pack
only what you really need
and not one thing more

and throughout the entire trip
no matter what the weather
you will always look
pressed and perfect.

I wish that you may inherit
the rosy gold of dawn
the sapphire blue of noon
and the diamond stars of velvet midnight.

May you
fall asleep
and dream
on a pillow
dappled with moonlight.

May you
turn a key
to open a door
that leads to
an attic
with a trunk
full of
laughing memories.

I wish for you
the silent melody
of handclasp,
the song of friendship
that needs no words.

I wish for you to have
a photograph album
expansive enough to contain
pictures of all
that you want to hold on to
in your life

all the sights and sounds
and tastes
of sweet and bittersweet
through the days and seasons
and years

all the faces and places
you want to recall
from the gentled past

and all that you hope to
run ahead to meet
in the sparkling unknown future

and I wish
most of all
that in your wondrous album
there will always be
a page for me.

Designed by Mary Tara O'Keefe
Type set in Garamond